R\
to S   ...o

by Jim O'Donnell

© Jim O'Donnell 2010

First Published 2010

The Royal Yachting Association
RYA House, Ensign Way
Hamble, Southampton SO31 4YA

Tel: 0845 345 0400

Fax: 0845 345 0329

E-mail: publications@rya.org.uk

Web: www.rya.org.uk

ISBN: 978 – 19064 35 – 400

RYA order code: G91

A CIP record of this book is available from the British Library.

Note: While all reasonable care had been taken in the preparation of this book, the publisher takes no responsibility for the use of the methods or products or contracts described in the book.

Cover and Typesetting: Jude Williams

Illustrations: Pete Galvin

Proofreading: Alan Thatcher

Printed: in China through World Print

Top Tips for Baiting Up

- Always use clean hands when handling bait. Scents from soaps, perfumes etc can transfer onto the bait and ruin its appeal to fish.
- Always use the freshest bait you can buy or find, most fish will only take fresh bait.
- Keep worm and fish baits fresh in a cool bag.
- Live crabs should be kept in a container with a lid – out of the sun.
- Keep baitfish alive by using a bait tank with an aerator.
- Ragworm can be kept for up to a week in a cool environment in a container lined with damp newspaper or peat. Check daily and remove any dead worms or they will contaminate the remaining live worms.
- Lugworm - rinse off any loose sand and store in a cool place on several layers of newspaper.
- You will have greater success if you always try to source baits local to the area you are fishing.
- Collecting your own bait can save you money.
- Try using bait elastic to secure difficult fish, crabs and shellfish baits onto the hook.
- Mount your bait onto the correct sized hook, if the bait obstructs the hook point you may not hook your fish or even worse lose it!
- Use a sharp knife to prepare baits – but be careful.
- Remember, all baits can carry harmful bacteria so always wash your hands after handling bait.

Protection of the environment

All the baits recommended in this book are abundant and sustainable. When you fish do not leave abandoned tackle that can harm animals and birds.

If possible, take dry refuse home to recycle.

TIGHT LINES...

Contents

King Ragworm *(nereis diversicolor)*

The largest of the ragworm family growing to over 45 cm (18 in) and as thick as your thumb. One of the most favoured sea anglers' baits as it catches most species and is readily available at tackle shops. Large worms can be used on their own and small worms bunched onto the hook. A great bait to use in a cocktail with other baits such as fish slithers and squid. **Status -** abundant.

Harbour rag (Maddies) is a smaller variety of ragworm so smaller hooks need to be used.

How to locate
In estuaries at low tide by digging up mud, shingle or shale. Sold in tackle shops by weight. Not suitable for home freezing.

Target Species
Bass, Bream, Dogfish, Flatfish, Plaice, Pollack, Ray, Sole, Whiting and Wrasse.

Hook Sizes
1 to 4/0.

How to use Ragworm

1 Grip the worm by the head and pass the point of the hook through the worm's mouth, then thread the hook down through the worm's body.
2 Bring the hook point back out through the side of the worm.
3 Thread any excess worm up the hook, over the eye and up the trace line.
4 Add more worms if needed.
5 Fish under a float, on a long flowing trace or on the seabed.

A single ragworm bait

Common Lugworm *(areniola marina)*

Also called the blow lug, a regular choice for estuaries and beaches especially in winter. A juicy bait full of scent with good fish attraction capabilities. Use large worms on their own or bunch small worms together. Makes great bait when mixed in a cocktail with other baits such as squid.

Status - abundant.

Black Lug can be used in the same way.

How to locate
At low tide by digging in muddy estuaries or sandy beaches. Sold live by weight in fishing tackle shops. Only black lug is suitable for home freezing.

Target Species
Bass, Cod, Dogfish, Flatfish, Plaice, Ray, Red Mullet, Sole, Whiting and Wrasse.

Hook Sizes
1/0 to 5/0.

How to use **Lugworm**

1 If you wish, remove the worm's tail allowing the scent to release quicker.
2 Grip the worm and pass the point of the hook through the tail, then thread the hook down through the worm's body.
3 Bring the hook point back out through the head end of the worm.
4 Thread any excess worm up the hook, over the eye and up the trace line.
5 Add more worms if needed.
6 Fish on a short trace on the seabed.

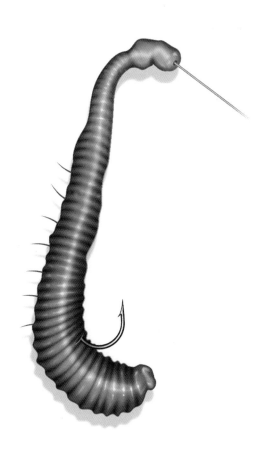

A single lugworm with tail removed

Hardbacks *(carcinus marinas)*

Common Shore Crabs (carcinus marinas) are found around beaches and rock pools in the UK and the coasts of northern Europe. Used live, they are a useful bait to target certain species of fish.

Status - abundant.

How to locate

At low tide, small crabs can be collected from under rocks, weed and other objects in estuaries and on rocky beaches. A crab the size of a 50p piece is the perfect size. Not available from tackle shops. Not suitable from home freezing.

Target Species

Bass, Gurnard, Smooth Hound and Wrasse

Hook Sizes

2/0 to 4/0.

How to use Hardback crabs

1 Remove the crab's claws – they can damage lines!
2 Push the hook through the crab's body and shell – behind the back legs.
3 Fish under a float or on the seabed.

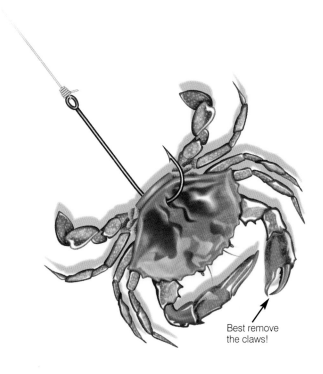

Best remove
the claws!

A hooked live hardback crab

Peeler Crab

Common Shore Crabs in moulting period and about to shed
the old shell in order to grow bigger and grow a new shell
(carapace). In this stage they are so pungent and juicy most
fish cannot resist them and a wide variety of fish species feed
specifically on them. Excellent when used in a cocktail of other
baits such as ragworm or lugworm.

Status - abundant.

How to locate
At certain times of the year crabs gather in estuaries in order to peel
and grow. At low tide gather from under rocks, weed and other objects.
Check it is ready by pulling off one of the crab's legs – if it bares white
sinew it is not ready – if it bears a new leg it is. Sold live (individually)
from some tackle shops. Suitable for home freezing.

Target Species
Bass, Cod, Dogfish, Flatfish, Plaice, Ray, Sole, Smooth Hound,
Whiting and Wrasse.

Hook Sizes
1/0 to 4/0.

How to use Peeler Crab

1 Remove the crab's legs.
2 Carefully remove the crab's shell.
3 Remove the crab's lungs (if you wish).
4 Thread the hook through the crab's body or through one leg socket
   and out of another.
5 Use bait elastic to secure the bait firmly on the hook.
6 Fish on a short trace on the seabed.

Use bait elastic to secure the crab to the hook

Molluscs

Squid *(loligo vulgaris)*

One of the most popular baits and can be used whole or cut into strips and added to a cocktail of baits. A great bait to attract big fish and is used in winter with lugworm.
Status - abundant.

How to locate
Almost impossible to catch. Readily available frozen in packs or boxes from tackle shops. Suitable for home freezing if you can catch them!

Target Species
Bass, Bream, Cod, Conger, Dogfish, Flatfish, Gurnard, Ling, Pollack, Ray, Tope and Whiting.

Hook Sizes
3/0 to 6/0.

How to use Squid

1 Whole on a large hook or Pennel rig (two hooks).
2 Cut into various sized strips and slithers.
3 Simply put or threaded onto the hook.
4 Secured with bait elastic to the hook.

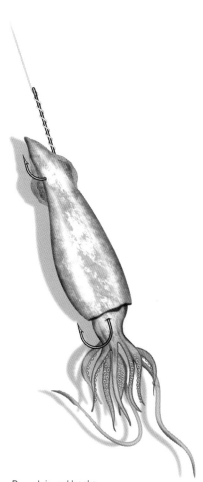

A whole squid on Pennel rigged hooks

Cuttlefish *(sepia officinalis)*

A mollusc and not a fish. Best used whole to catch big fish. For
smaller fish use as strips or slithers.
Status · abundant.

How to locate

Almost impossible to catch but are readily available frozen in packs
from tackle shops. Suitable for home freezing. However, they do not
re-freeze well so only take sufficient for your trip.

Target Species

Bass, Cod, Conger, Ling, Rays and Tope.

Hook Sizes

4/0 to 8/0.

How to use Cuttlefish

1 Can be used whole on a large hook or on a Pennel rig (two hooks).

2 Can be cut into strips and slithers of various sizes.

3 Simply put or thread onto the hook.

4 Fish on the seabed.

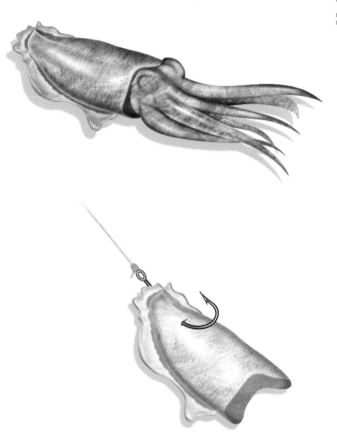

Whole cuttlefish on a big hook

Sandeels *(ammodytes tobianus)*

A great summer bait for a wide variety of fish. Can be used live or dead and fished under a float in mid water or on the seabed.
Status - abundant.

How to locate

Not an easy one to catch! Found by digging specific sandy beaches at low tide. Readily available frozen in packs from most tackle shops and live from some. Often worth checking with local fishing skippers, if you are lucky they may sell you some.

Keep live sandeels in an aerated bait tank. When freezing at home it is best to freeze them individually, which speeds up freezing (and unfreezing) and makes baiting easier. Do this by laying them on a tray, once frozen they can be bagged in trip size packs.

Target Species

Bass, Cod, Dogfish, Flatfish, Garfish, Mackerel, Pollack and Rays.

Hook Sizes

1/0 to 4/0.

How to use Sandeels

1 Dead – by threading onto a hook (a bit like a worm) using bait elastic to secure to the hook.
2 Live – hook through the eye.

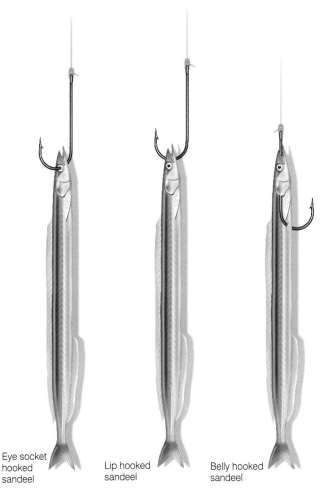

Eye socket
hooked
sandeel

Lip hooked
sandeel

Belly hooked
sandeel

Launce – Greater Sandeel
(hyperoplus lanceolatus)

Can grow to 30cm (12 inches) and irresistible to almost every species of fish. A good bait to use dead or live in summer.
Status - abundant.

How to locate
Can be caught using feathers over offshore reefs and sandbanks. Also available frozen in packs from fishing tackle shops. Keep live launce in a live bait tank. Suitable for home freezing.

Target Species
Bass, Cod, Flatfish, Pollack and Rays.

Hook Sizes
4/0 to 6/0.

How to use Launce

1 Dead – thread (see page 16) onto a single or a double hook and use bait elastic to secure firmly on the hook.
2 Live – hook through the top of the snout – make sure it is secure!
3 Fish on a long flowing trace under a float or on the seabed.

A lip hooked live launce

Mackerel

The most widely used and versatile of baits and can be used dead or live, whole, cut or slithered. There is hardly a species of fish that does not eat mackerel! Garfish or herring are a poor substitute as they are not as oily or attractive. Great to use in a cocktail of baits.

Status - abundant.

How to locate
Available frozen in packs from tackle shops or by weight from fishmongers and the fish counter of most supermarkets. One of the easiest and exciting fish to catch and the first fish ever caught by a lot of anglers. Catch on land from piers, rocks and beaches by using a feathered trace or float. From a boat using feathers. Suitable for home freezing.

Target Species
Bass, Bream, Cod, Conger, Dogfish, Flatfish, Garfish, Ling, Mackerel, Pollack, Rays and all species of Shark.

Hook Sizes
1/0 to 8/0.

How to use Mackerel

1 Dead
  (a) Whole
  (b) Flappered – fish on the seabed only.
  (c) Fillet
  (d) Cut into chunks
  (e) Cut into slithers

2 Live – by hooking through the upper jaw. Fish on a long flowing trace under a float or on the seabed.

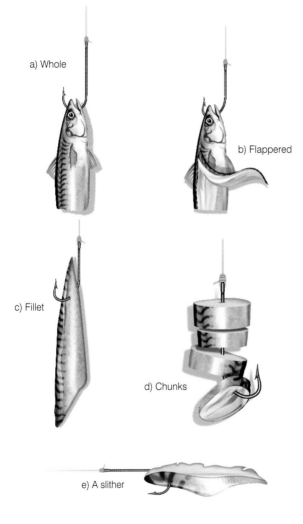

a) Whole

b) Flappered

c) Fillet

d) Chunks

e) A slither

Prawns

A good bait used dead (uncooked) for winter fishing when crabs and other baits are scarce. Have great appeal to some species of fish.

Status - abundant.

How to locate

Available frozen in packs from some fishing tackle shops or fresh from a fishmonger. They can be netted live from harbours, piers and rocks. Suitable for home freezing.

Target Species

Bass, Bream, Dogfish, Garfish, Mackerel, Pollack and Wrasse.

Hook Sizes

1/0 to 3/0.

How to use Prawns

1 Dead – thread onto the hook as for a worm.

2 Live – hook through the tip of the tail.

3 Method – fish under a float or on the seabed.

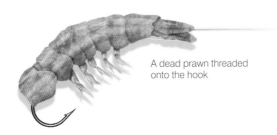

A dead prawn threaded
onto the hook

A tail hooked live prawn

Shellfish

There is a wide variety available which make great baits, and include razorfish, limpets, mussels and clams. These baits are fished almost like crab and used in winter when peeler crab is scarce. Make a good cocktail when used with worms.
Status - abundant.

Target Species
Bass, Bream, Cod, Dogfish, Flatfish, Whiting and Wrasse.

Hook Sizes
1/0 to 4/0.

How to use Shellfish

1 Remove all shellfish from their shells.
2 Place whole on the hook and use bait elastic to secure the bait firmly onto the hook.
3 Fish on the seabed.

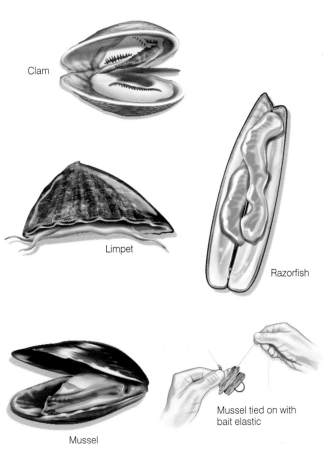

Clam

Limpet

Razorfish

Mussel

Mussel tied on with
bait elastic

Hard Artificial Baits
(hard plastic plug lures)

Designed to replicate a live fish and come in a wide variety of shapes, sizes and colours. Some float on the surface while others dive to a predetermined depth for example:

- subsurface
- floating divers
- sinking divers
- deep divers.

The species you are targeting along with the area will help you decide which type you should use. Work best in depths of up to 15 metres (50 feet) and are especially good for predatory fish cruising the upper waters.

Target Species
Bass, Garfish, Mackerel and Pollack.

Hook Sizes
Usually pre-fitted.

How to use Hard Artificial Baits

1 Choose which lure you require, depending on the depth you intend to fish. Surface baits float on the surface. Shallow divers dive to approximately 2 metres (six feet). Deep divers dive to in excess of 3 metres (ten feet).

2 Attach the lure to the mainline, cast and retrieve by turning the fishing reel handle.

3 To add extra action to the lure, vary the speed you retrieve and try twitching the rod tip.

A deep diving plug

A shallow diving plug

A surface popping plug

Soft Artificial Baits (soft rubber lures)

Designed to look like live bait fish when being retrieved. They are available in lots of shapes, sizes and colours. Almost all are designed to sink and they usually come with an integral weight. Good for predatory species that feed in mid-water or on the seabed.

Target Species
Bass, Coalfish, Cod, Ling and Pollack.

Hook Sizes
3/0 to 8/0 if not pre-fitted.

How to use Soft Artificial Baits

1 Small light baits can be cast using a rod and the same principles as hard artificial baits (page 26) .

2 Larger heavier artificial baits are used to fish deeper waters and should be attached with additional weight to a flowing rig. Drop the lure to the seabed and retrieve to either the depth you wish to fish at, or to the surface – use the reel to do this!

3 Add extra action by twitching the top of the rod and by varying the retrieval speed.

Jelly worm

Rubber eel

Shad

Pirks, Jigs, Spinners & Spoons

Metal lures which look similar to bait fish or squid and are available in a huge variety of sizes and colours. The shininess of the metal helps attract fish and the vibration in the water can replicate an injured fish. All are designed to sink and they are excellent for predatory fish that feed deep in the water or on the seabed.

Target Species

Pirks and Jigs – Bass, Coalfish, Cod, Ling and Pollack.

Spinners and Spoons – Bass, Garfish, Mackerel, and Pollack.

Hook Sizes

Usually pre-fitted.

How to use **Pirks, Jigs, Spinners and Spoons**

1 **Pirks and Jigs** – used to fish deep water. Attach the lure to the mainline. Drop the lure to the seabed and retrieve to the surface, or a predetermined height above the seabed, by turning the fishing reel handle. Jerk the lure to make it life-like.

2 **Spinners and Spoons** – attached direct to the mainline. Cast and retrieved using the reel handle. To add extra action to the lure, vary the speed you retrieve and try twitching the rod tip.

Pirk lure

Jig

Spinner lure